I've long been drawn to poets whose works—defined by precision, by transcendence—create moments of intense possibility in uncovering the exquisite nature of the ordinary. James Owens is one of them. His writing deftly mingles all lyrical and narrative threads into bursts of vision, beauty, clarity—wholly remarkable and singular. Owens is a poet who carries, in the words of Alan Tate, "the secret wisdom around the world"—placing his work firmly in the lineage of Virgil to Donne to Elizabeth Bishop, Paul Celan, Charles Wright, Kathryn Stripling Byer.

In *Family Portrait with Scythe*, his latest book, Owens writes of relationships and place—in striking blends of Appalachia, northern Indiana, Ontario, in a scattering of histories—with a fixated need for all truths hidden in the land—its deep veins of coal and death, its skies full of silent birds, its riverbanks always revealing something new. The voices in these poems are convincing, familiar, and thoroughly bent to mission: "I walked on, heavy, and carried this only world" (from "Last Thoughts Cooling Like an Abandoned Cup"). Their stories compel the poet and stir the reader, as in the stunning "Imagine a Woman Behind Razor Wire": "you must tell it speak it write it." This collection may unsettle your ease, but that's what it was meant to do.

—Sam Rasnake, author of *Cinéma Vérité*
and editor of *Blue Fifth Review*

These poems have a crystalline economy and startling depths, whether they begin with a "vast autumn flock of birds," lovers in the rain, or a marriage coming apart. Even as he laments the trials and losses of existence, James Owens insists that if we remember joy, we must "tell it speak it write it." He invites us to delight in the things of this world, which now include this luminous book.

—Jeff Gundy, author of *Without a Plea*

OTHER BOOKS BY JAMES OWENS

Loan of the Quick (chapbook), The Sow's Ear Press, 1998.
An Hour is the Doorway, Black Lawrence, 2007.
Frost Lights a Thin Flame, Mayapple Press, 2007.
Mortalia, Future Cycle Press, 2015.

FAMILY PORTRAIT WITH SCYTHE

JAMES OWENS

HARMONY SERIES

BOTTOM DOG PRESS

HURON, OHIO

ISBN:978-1-947504-20-2
Bottom Dog Press, Inc.
PO Box 425, Huron, OH 44839
Lsmithdog@aol.com
http://smithdocs.net

CREDITS:
General Editor: Larry Smith
Cover & Layout Design: Susanna Sharp-Schwacke
Front Cover Art: *Song of the Lark*, by Winslow Homer

CONTENTS

PART FOUR: ONTARIO

For my wife, Erin,

and for my mother, Charlotte.

BURN

The house inhaled and roared, as burning gripped
and pummeled every plank and ancient nail,
the moss-splotched roof sagging deeply, windows
boarded blind, the yard all weeds and brier.
The fire made its own weather out of heat.
It drew the frozen air of a winter night
and changed it, smudged it, which rose as smoke,
and lofted sparks in trails. The burning house
cast flame-light over the wooded swale below,
trees' leafless skeletons as stark and black
as geometric drawings on thin snow,
as the fire surged and shifted, and no one
down there to look up at the strange red sky.
except rabbits and a fox or screech owl.
It was the kind of night when frost breaks stones,
the cold at my back a steel plate, heat pushing
my chest like the forbidding palm of God.
I stared into the fire, the furnace of rooms
where living had once been possible. Listen,
what makes this a story is that something
called me in. A few steps more, and I might
dissolve in light and a cleansing
pain. I swear to you, it sounded good.
I almost went, before I turned and drove
on through unwatching dark and let that house
collapse to ash. If I had chosen to burn,
I couldn't tell you now. Telling is the point.

PART ONE

LASCAUX

LASCAUX

The chubby boy who dreams of dogs: a pack
of slat-ribbed, fever-eyed strays, snapping mouths
raw with mange. Hemmed in, no running back
or forward on the mud path behind the house,
a cramped passage between the weedy hill
too steep for escape and a hopeless blank wall
of tar-paper siding. As they slouch in for the kill,
he swings a broken stick but is slow and small.

Often, he faces the dogs. Then the night a horse
steps into his room, nothing funny, uncombed mane,
hooves strange on the floor, moving like a horse
toward the bed. He tastes an open vein
of fear spilled in his throat. He thinks he is awake
and dreads revelation, knowing the horse will speak.

CARNAGE

The weasel knew their warmth in the dark,
ripped throats, let drop the gangly,

earnest bodies of two-week-old domer chicks
we found slain in the obvious morning light,

the chicken coop an aftermath, an abattoir,
blood-sopping tufts of down scattered awry,

forty-eight of fifty dead, the two living birds
huddled in a corner, heads under their wings.

My tender mother falls to her knees.
She can't erase their fear in those jaws.

My father tries what he cannot do,
beside her on the dew-beaded grass,

arms around her heaving shoulders,
promising more chicks, a better coop,

saying her name, touching her face,
both of them uncomprehending and bloodied,

words too frail in the gap as she pulls away.

THE NEWS, C. 1969

Winter evenings, a spot reddened on the flank
of the cast-iron stove. Heat bulged into the room
when my grandfather leaned to the open door to hock
coal dust and blood, or spat tobacco juice
on the fat black belly, where it
sizzled and popped and thickened like tar.

Silence was the command for visiting children,
as helicopters *whup-whupped* over jungle where soldiers
slumped around a crater or swelled in bags,
while generals argued escalation, the TV staging
riots and splashdowns in places
whose names we couldn't have spun
off a globe, Birmingham or Cape Canaveral
as distant as Saigon, Nixon as foreign as Mao.

Snow fell in the windows, veiling the gouged hills.
We were far from it all, as he broke his own rule
of unfooled attention to the world's happenings
and turned to us, pointing a flattened, coal-rimmed nail
at *The Huntley-Brinkley Report*:
"Listen, if any of you'uns wants to be something,
you better learn to talk like them lying sons-of-bitches."

SLEDGE

We learned at work what lightness owes to craft.
The tug of iron on joints weighing the real
eased when balanced rightly, levered and deft,
and it paid to track the grain, before a blow
would crack the knee-high chunks of oily coal
to fit a stove-door. Swung wrong, the recoil
of mishandled strength would ring wrist and elbow,
jarring the hammer back from that still unbroken,
matte-black surface. Useless the planted heel,
the over-muscled swing. It took a feel
for the clever angle, percussive *tonk* that opened
dull coal to primeval gloss, as the slabs fell
apart to the kindest tap—not force, but known
and managed heft, gravity aimed and owned.

SCYTHE

My father fought incursions of pigweed, bindweed,
and purple loosestrife. As the blades of lesser tools
thinned and snapped from use, he repaired hoes
and hatchets and spades and released them to any hand,

but the scythe was his alone, a man's deadly implement
that, swung stupidly, would open a leg to the wet bone.
It glowered from its pegs on the shed wall,
shaft crooked to ease the work, cracked from weather,

handles polished as pleasurable as skin with the oils
of labor. The dark crescent of steel glinted
along its edge in the dimness, attractive but forbidden
for boys prone to stumble in their ignorant gravity.

I remember plain work done as it should be done,
the hand's or eye's love for the angle tapped true,
the clean hole dug square, the measured cut.
He sat cross-legged at the base of a slope too steep

and rock-bound for machines and plied a file in
curt strokes that raised a sharpness on the blade.
Then up, leaning into his own spun center, a wide-elbowed,
flow-hipped rhythm that snicked stems an inch

above the soil, the scythe seemingly as without effort
as light bending through water, he laid thistles and briers
in long swathes, to be raked in mounds and to dry
for the sweet smoke of fires that marked cleared ground.

FAMILY PORTRAIT WITH SCYTHE

My father was smaller and emptier,
wearing some never-spoken,
embarrassed apology, regret

like a battered mask. He spent
many nights away from home,
fishing, or saying he was fishing.

My mother tired herself
in the garden, weeding and canning.
Neither offered a word to me

about what had passed
that drove them to sleep alone,
an old-fashioned propriety

toward words spoken
or flung behind bedroom doors
keeping both reticent,

and me nineteen and heartless,
too rapt with the puzzle
of myself to care to ask.

Summers had been the raspberry
harvest, always handfuls to eat,
bucketfuls to preserve for pies

and jams, sweetness for every winter.
This year was different.
When the berries weighted

the raspberry canes
like the clotted blood
of some vast animal

that had wandered unwisely
into their tangles and thrashed out,
my father took the scythe

and hacked briers and berries
all equally to the earth,
for the fruit to rot or feed birds

and for the debris to burn
in autumn brush fires.
My mother gave no sign of surprise,

no reproach, perhaps relieved
to let it all go, to see
anger that might mean his survival.

Later, after much has happened,
when my lonely wife
frowns at me across a table

and says she doesn't know
what should happen next,
knowing secretly

that this will translate
into lives apart,
I understand—as if she has bent

a wire to complete a circuit
that has lain open for twenty years—
my father's embarrassment

when I came home that summer,
when he had no choice
but admit sadness and failure,

his repudiation by time.
I have no scythe to whet
and heave against berry canes,

but for that year and the next,
everywhere I go, I wear
my father's apology, like a mask.

FUNERAL

The boy waited out the afternoon, sifting
palmfuls of sun-glinting road dust on the heads

of soldiers—disaster, a caving dune
on their desert expedition beneath the hot sky—

and waited for his father, at last, still black
from the mine, not too tired then to chase a boy

laughing to a fall on the grass, scuffing
cheeks with his coal grit and daylong sweat,

his muscular breath before going in
to lather thick as fat in the basement shower.

The boy watched this ritual: his father
sluicing work from back and heavy arms,

who shuddered later to pull the hardened air,
who lies stilled here and pale, is no one now.

Last Thoughts Cooling like an Abandoned Cup
– i.m. Jack Owens, 1936-2003

1.
I must have dozed. And found him watching day
describe spring's imperfect unrest
from his pillow, starlings unskeining, blown astray
over open furrows, until the fist in his chest
spasmed, the next hacking fit wrung blood
and soot from his raw throat. He spat red grief
in a cloth and winked to say he understood
what I knew, too. The end would be relief.

"Torment after this and fire forever, I guess
that's bullshit," he rasped—asking, paying breath
to ask. And I: "Bullshit. What God would bless
with one hand, while the other tortures his dead?"
He nodded, half-smiled, slept. I paced his bedside,
unquiet as hollow ground, unsure if I'd lied.

2.
He called again, just days before he died.
"I can't breathe, Jimmy," he panted, though no one
had called me Jimmy since I became a man.
"My throat feels stuffed tight with lint. I could cry
for one real breath of good air." It was late.
My wife was working. More work awaited me.
Our sleepless two-year-old crawled around my feet.
Vague wind fumbled between us in the dark states.

"That's rough. I'm sorry to hear it," I tried,
ashamed, already, for the harried note,
the awkward pause. But he chose the odd moments,
as if, long awake and stumped for words at night,
he knew the weight of unbalanced accounts
that should be righted, though impossible to right.

3.
Death was so far from upheaval, the cup
of coffee balanced on his knee did not spill.
Perhaps his final breath or failing scrap
of dream cast tremors across the little pool
of dark. Would dying then have surprised him,
his chest veined with Pall Malls and coal,
one lung left, a gray mitt, gripping the slim
shaft of air? Might he have known and let go?

His wife came into the room. She said "Jack"
and touched his shoulder, thinking him asleep,
and then she knew. She stood, suddenly calm,
as spring breathed at the window, lifted the cup
like a small animal's slain heart—again, "Jack"—
and held it, warmth soaking into her palms.

4.
As neurons failed, he lost the big plow horse
that broke his wrist when he was eight years old,
the forbidden gallop across stubble and frost
worth the hurt for the joy of that shining ride;
the first, secret and primal time he learned
the shocking gush of semen; the entire year
he and a buddy hitched to Florida; the burn
of moonshine; dogs and hunts, night and fire;

whether the cherry blossoms he cut for my mother
as she was weeping ached, too light in his embrace;
my sleepy weight, when he came stale with beer
to scoop me from bed and nuzzle my face,
spent from a bender, begging entry, and me his shield,
he deflecting her just wrath by holding his child.

5.
An ordinary grave that smelled like a ditch,
like any other. In sunlight. An April day
when new leaves already gleamed like patches
of silk that lived on the old leaves' decay.
The pain that clogged his chest with dust had died.
We sat on plastic chairs and glanced toward
the mound of dirt that would fall back in to hide
his box. Like headache, the blur of holy words.

I punched him once, in play—first he laughed,
daring me at twelve to show if I could hit,
then, shocked, my knuckles on his teeth, lip split,
he staggered back a step and rubbed his mouth,
spat blood, and hunched away. And now the sorrow
of that blow is in my fist and beats me hollow.

6.
The shrew was not his valedictory ghost.
I wanted to lie and drain myself from myself,
so hard it was to parse out spring from grief.
The wind died down and rose again, almost
as if a hand had roughed the grass and crossed
where banks of violet and renewed twinleaf
flaked light off air. I needed but damned relief,
and walked alone in woods, and walked to be lost.

Leaf litter rustled. A humble thing, the shrew,
and oddly unafraid, came straight as a herald
across the path and nosed around my shoe
but left no message and sought the weather-gnarled
roots of an oak. Too wild or wise to call it true,
I walked on, heavy, and carried this only world.

7.
If we meet, it will be in some mine's solid dark,
timbers popping as the roof settles, and I'll know
by his blackened face in the helmet light's glow
how far he has traveled since death has done its work,
how much forgotten, of life and love and work,
when he smiles vaguely, unsure. "I used to like
the high ridgetops, where you felt you could fly....
I know you...." I move to him—but the rest is dark,

so I borrow from Virgil: *"Give me your hand,*
father, do not draw back from my embrace."
He spoke thus, tears flooding his grateful face.
Three times there he tried to link his arms around
that neck, but the vainly held shade, every time,
fled on the empty air, a flitting dream.

8.
I was best man at my father's wedding, before
the cancer gnawed him thin. He looked like *his*
father, nervous in a new jacket, but sure.
I met his new wife, saw her sneak him a kiss,
who had softened the place with a few rugs,
woman's knickknacks. When the preacher said so,
I gave him the ring, then a rare, brief, last hug,
and we were two ordinary men, letting go.

I have a wrinkled photograph of him as a boy,
before his wives and many years before me,
where he faces the world with an uncomplicated look,
nothing to forgive. I'm old enough to be his father,
so I'd hold that yet unharrowed body, gather
him unembarassed in my arms, and rock.

The Prodigal Son Makes Notes for a Eulogy
and Never Mentions the Fatted Calf

I write around the borders of some territory
we have lived our lives in sight of and never crossed.

What else can anyone do, except grope unlighted
around the edges of loss and fumble to describe

the intricate gap, like the blind who depend on touch
to know a face? In the American myths, a boy

born to hard circumstance, but smarter or more resourceful
or more ruthless, will rise to wrest himself from history

and genetics and geography. But what about an ordinary boy,
born into coal dust, suckled from the weary veins of the Depression?

What life except his own life? Can we love the hidden things?
How to choose detail? It all glittered. It all disappeared.

Fragments shattered, clattering, caught in the throat of his dying
memory. Is it in the common dirt that we know each other finally?

There was a Christmas morning in the sixties. I sat warm
as he held me, and he, who could hardly read, read

from the new book of stories. I will try to recall other things to tell you,
but writing it can only fail, and now there is only the writing it.

I could stitch my own myth of the man from story and archetype—
and what else does anyone have? does any son think he has more?—

but I would rather lose him than remember lies. Loss is real and heavy
and as hard to carry and balance as a shuttle of slack coal,

but loss is better than falsification. Is that true? It had better be,
as I say his name above this hollowed earth and you say it back.

Waking Beside a Scene from *The Inferno*

The slate dump breathes hell and rotten eggs,
unfinished as lust, little twirls of smoke

from some fire in its guts the spring rain
can't reach, that twist and thin as they rise

through the last panels of chill darkness,
breath forgetting the body of rock and slag.

He finds himself here again, unsurprised,
a half-mile down the swerving road from his bed

where the window's rainy daylight wakes alone.
Forms hulk and blur in this dawn of slow drizzle,

and he is drawn helplessly to this final landscape,
as if the acres of smoldering cinder, the hopeless slough

of black mire where a creek sickened on runoff,
the broken, rusting machinery cast away here,

answer some stripped hillside in him that he must climb.
The world is a far, bright circle of sun behind wet cloud.

The men in the trucks go past without smiling,
mouths set on the day's work, or turning to cough loss

into the slanting rain, faces gray from their war
with money, bloodstains like slashes on handkerchiefs.

Morning blackens in his mouth. The roar
of heavy traffic shudders up through the steering wheel,

coal dust and sulfur ash thick in the wiper swathes,
thick in the throat, sifting soft in the lungs.

Story

1.

My mother's voice deepens into trance—it is a winter evening, the wind
shushing its dry dust of new snow across the already fallen and packed
snow under the matter-of-fact illumination of the porch light, when I
look out to gauge the weather, a visiting middle-aged son—

and she tells me how my great-grandfather killed two men over a woman—this
was eastern Kentucky in the 1890s and he a scion of the hot decades
before, his father a leader on the McCoy side of the feud—over a
woman

who was really a girl but who knew herself, my mother insists, as black-haired as
night and her body rich with some admixture of Cherokee blood, or
what darker blood they claimed was Cherokee then,

one of the men killed to have the woman, the other, his own cousin, tricked
with a fake letter pretending to be a summons from the woman and
bushwhacked because he knew of the first killing and would use the
knowledge, not in service of some abstract justice, but for wedge and
profit.

2.

And forty years later, my mother's mother, who had married into that bloodline—

those archetypal figures of Old Testament absoluteness stripping themselves
bare on the earth to be damned, knowing and defiant, and whose
histories moved always like palpable shades through my childhood,
figures of the nineteenth century, of the Civil War and after, the
cauldron of slaughter and of avarice lust pride rage—

my grandmother heard the story from the woman herself, still then tall and
unbent and deigning neither pride nor shame, who even pointed out
the two hidden graves that had birthed from her thighs like full-grown
children smelling of the broken earth,

warning that silence was best while the still dangerous old man lived, her husband.

3.

And always and yet—my mother near seventy now, thin and gray as a handful
of sticks but the seep of their blood still a pulse somewhere in her,
like fingertips marking echo on taut skin, drawing her back to the
inescapable stories, their starved gravity envious of the present warmth
and light—

that time past holding its precedence over time now, as if it could judge and
condemn not the rightness or wrongness of any action but the laxness
of passion, the pallor of our anger or of insufficient greed for more
life that pounded in them forever at the forge-bright core of desire,

as the past like a distended membrane containing faces and hands in a broth of
words bulges into the darkening, star-refulgent winter night of one
hundred and twenty years after the act,

my mother's voice continuing in the known grooves, a fascinated retracing of
fracture in the foundations. And somehow—she is stunned to realize it—

4.

only she and now I are left of all those once living and long dead to carry the
truth, what truth there still is, as part-forgotten and part-invented as it
must be by now, in the shaping exigency

of these innumerable tellings and the need of memory to recall some shape
even to that which has been lost forever,

and therefore not lost but changed, transmuted into a truth superior to the
random attrition of detail.

5.

Later, I will lie in the dim quiet of my childhood bed in the room that survived
my childhood and still cradles its small collection of items past the
wreckage of time,

frost paling in latticed curves on the windowpanes as the moon rises,

and the fox my great-grandmother knew on such nights will come to the edge
      of the woods on the hillside above the house, snug in his thick winter
      fur, precise feet tracking in a single line the crusted surface, warmth
      floating around his muzzle in the figures of condensing breath,

and will call his whetted hunger over and over into the cold and laden air.

To Cleave

If you can forget yourself in precision,
the stove-lengths of raw-scented poplar
will fall without effort, slabs of bright wood

opening to the autumn afternoon,
less work than a reminder of the earth.
Hold this satisfaction against decay:

a private rite, violence gentled in the palms,
play of muscle and joint, sleek weight
of an ax handle sensuous from long use.

An old woman died, who lay three seasons
in pain undimmed by morphine, breath dragging
her chest with a ragged wetness, cancers budding

her womb like toadstools in a discarded cradle.
You left her house back into the tumbled
abundance of October, surprised at the sun,

her trees dingy with the year's progress.
Now you spend a day out of this very year
splitting firewood for the coming winter,

which is more than a metaphor for death,
because it is the reality of death
repeated in the body of time. Wood falls

in usable chunks, and you stack them
in waist-high rows. She rots underground.
But swing the ax again, hungry for impact,

numb-fingered with need for force and heft.
The injured move this way sometimes,
as if the broken bone will heal, the horrible furrow

in flesh stitch itself to a pale seam of scar—
or the way an explorer searches out a path
into an unpeopled valley, gripping his ax,

weary, tracking the scent of fresh water
down slopes of tangled vine to the sun-washed pools
that must be there, ahead
                              through uncut woods.

PART TWO

THE DISCOVERY OF BREAD

A Prayer for Unison

When my scattered longings rise to go, let it be
as if at dawn one of these vast autumn flocks

of starlings has paused to liven our maples
with lilt and chatter, and to stand beneath the trees

is to coalesce at the stem of an intricate,
now waking, dark brain as it thinks

of itself. The birds shift with never a rest
from branch to branch, tree to tree,

taking off and darting an arc out over
the road and homing back, sometimes

a dozen or so patrolling in formation
above the dim yard, the whirr of their wings

in tune as they pass. And each is separate,
a nerve firing into motion that seems random,

while the flock is still a unified being,
a mind aware within its subtle radius,

so that when it is time, all silence their chattering
to rise in a whispery rush and leave as one

into the brightening, airy spaces over the earth.

LOOKING BACK

The afterlife, if there is one,
will be like the window

when you are out here in the dark,
where you've come to investigate

a noise and have found
yourself so perplexed by stars

that you are strange now
under the vastness, and you turn

and see that things have kept
their shapes and relations,

like the parts of a sentence
that ought to be clear,

the lamp still on in there,
right where you left it,

the book tented on the arm
of the chair, the woman

coming down the stairs.
Her expression says

she is wondering what
has become of you, not

worried yet, not afraid.
She is probably your wife.

Hard Rain Behind a Screen of Thistles

If I remembered a story about rain, would that be a way back?
It was not this mean spring cold seeping under the doors
but a summer cloudburst when we stopped the car,
obeying the ache that twisted through our nerves that year,
and touched naked on the rich grass, secret
behind a row of thistle and clotted blackberry.
Rainwater was the taste of July sky licked from your thighs,
sopping our hair, streaming off your breasts, off my shoulders.

Later, in the afternoon, after watching more rain fall,
I think I should have said it was like a baptism.
Seeing us there, discovering those two hidden in the long grass,
would it seem that our whole bodies were weeping
the fat warm rain, movements tensing fast to a shared cry
lost in thunder, our bellies together, as slick as newborns?

Nights at 7-Eleven

My one overnight shift every seven days was quiet,
cleaning and stocking, toting up the purchases
of the truckers who passed through at three a.m.
or of university kids still drunk from a party.
During lulls, I would stand in the cool outside
the bright-windowed store, watching headlights
turn into taillights speeding toward D.C.
I got to know the bored cops who came in to chat.
Once a woman bought gum and flashed
her breasts on the way out, turning shy and tender
as she offered one on her palm like a plea.
The guy from the bakery unloaded fresh doughnuts
at five, when the sky was bleeding violet,
and birds were tuning up in the boxwood hedges.
I would carry home a bag of day-old pastries,
if good ones were left, cheese Danish and bear claws
and lemon long johns. Nothing wrong with them.
I walked. It wasn't far along the highway,
grainy sleepiness pleasantly weighting my limbs,
everything else waking, cars blowing past.
Then I climbed stairs to our apartment.
My first wife—what children we were,
wondering where to lodge our best devotions—
was yawning and dressing for her job
at the mall, and, before spending the day
apart, we sat close in the shadowy kitchen,
eating free doughnuts and making plans,
because we thought our real lives would begin soon,
fascinated with how the years caught
and reflected curious gleams, as we turned
the sugary future in our hands.

ABUNDANCE

As the bowl fills up with summer's sweetness,
there is an intensity to the world's
distillation of good in ripening blackberries
that you would like to call the land's intent.

It isn't. But at the end of a day in July,
the first sparse, syncopating drops of rain
whispering thin trails down through cooked air,
the temptation to believe stirs around you.

True enough, bumpy, finger joint-sized berries
are like the darkened nipples of a nursing mother,
but notice once that the lithe canes coil
like whips, and the proffered berries will congeal

to dark clots of old blood along the lashes,
dangerous with thorn and staining the fingers
equally well with juice or living hurt.
Meaning is much in the choice of figure,

but elected meaning is not the sun-warmed
burst of taste tongued behind your teeth,
which is the same for saints and murderers,
the same today and twenty years ago.

Some snake inhabits this rocky ground,
parchment scraps of shed skin caught on thorns.
Its whip-like length waits in hiding
to scrape surprisingly warm against your ankle

and send you recoiling. Black snake or copperhead,
like the earth's thin tongue to flick your knee?
You go forward not knowing, twisting berries,
braving the briar patch's empty threat or venom.

Now the rain comes harder. You start losing
the berries in darkness, so turn to the house
and the woman who will share this harvest,
picking your way back from the snake's palisade.

A few scratches burn, balanced by the weight
of the bowl in your hand, the promise of pleasure.
A good year: you leave fistfuls of berries behind,
not enough pies and jams anywhere to save them all.

BODY

1.
This violation. I left you at the door,
but passing your basement window, I saw—
an accident, but I lingered.

Unbuttoning, private and practical,
without ceremony, you tossed your skirt
to the bed and stretched for pleasure
in bra and panties before the mirror and half-
swiveled your hips, flexing
to appraise the sleek-muscled calf and your silken
firm thigh, happy and secret.

It was winter and late.
I trudged home,
my breath clinging to the air, flush
with the good story of the body.

2.
Those last nights before I left, when you undressed
behind the closet door so I would not see,
we slept in the same bed, but meticulously
measured our separate spaces, keeping to what was ours,
the edges of the mattress, avoiding dangerous touch.

Often those mornings, we woke tangled
together, the foolish bodies still dreaming of us,
the summer morning light washing the bed
like cool water that we refused.

Wanting a Storm on His Birthday

He desires wind itself above the house,
not wind as metaphor, as if a river
of days slides across the sky,

spiraling dust and the stiff leaves
of a dry November, the year's pivot
where air catches and is torn.

The warm lover sleeps beside him,
but he thinks of unresting clouds
and steps through heavy rooms.

The hour threatens, and he augurs
rain and lashed branches stripped
wild all through the dark country;

and he wants morning, glossed and wet,
twigs from the ruined choirs,
renewal and homecoming.

He wants to think about wind, not
the end hunting him from blind sky,
chasing his known years into chaos

like a flock of panicked starlings
when the hawk plummets hooked
and holy among their cries.

Light Whispers Through the Skin of the World
— for Ingrid, whom you remember

At the riverbank, it is dawn, or it is dusk,
blushing like a plain confession
that wisely avoids "light" and "whispers"
and isn't sure one can say anything
about "the world," though the ghost of wanting to
is still restless in the bramble and sloughs

like mist off the surface of the water. It has been
a long time since you thought you understood,
so long that you might not recognize clarity,
if you saw it stripped bare of language.
Memory goes back far, but not all the way,
not even all your own life, and what it favors

is random or irrelevant or hard to interpret.
You once read that the simplest organisms
have the most accurate perceptions, free
from the glimmer and sludge of thinking.
If a skittish doe came to drink, you would look
into her eyes with no idea what she is seeing

There are beetles that drag bubbles of air
beneath the water, like lenses they live in.
What do they see, when you stand here moping?
Of even greater privilege, are the mussels
that lash themselves to the sides of rocks
and filter what comes, inflow and outflow,

so they know only matter and force
and think nothing of it. A mussel's life
might not be as you imagine. How solitary
they are in their clusters of shells,
how timeless. We are different, we think.
Remember, all the way back, all

the way back in first grade, you knew a girl
named Ingrid, a pretty girl with long dark hair
and delicate hands—and she is somewhere now,
just as altered as you are—but you recall
the day she brought a fine-looking slice of
blackberry pie for lunch and ate it at her desk.

KATABASIS WITH A PHOTOGRAPH OF TWO CHILDREN

Knowing this turgid bumbler's teary bafflement will cease,
this sloppy, warm knot of blood and longing and regret
will slack and unravel in cooling ash or the cold pit,
that this absurd creature will end, is comfort and release,

but that these two—here twelve and eight, mugging at ease
for the camera, as if their miraculous bodies will not forget
our few days of leveraged peace, the summer cabin sunlit
and separate like the only emblem of my only grace—

knowing they will die, or worse, tremble in fear of death,
as they will and soon enough, I would beat to shards the stone
that frames this swindling world, would trade for their one more breath

this yet strong body and all the years still to weigh it down,
would damn any god for hurt to come and drag the sky down,
would howl in dark hell, where my father has gone before me down.

LINDISFARNE

1.
A limited freedom in this secured space,
like a soldier's hand in a wired gauntlet.
I walk from room to room and wait.
For something. Every Thursday morning
the garbage trucks rumble past
like a military maneuver, those devourers,
and every afternoon my daughter
trudges back from school, smiling
—a bit distracted, it seems—at the dogs
restrained by the neighbors' fences, at the drifts
of snow, her mind somewhere else,
though the little cage of her supple bones
comes home. I wanted for years
to translate Alcuin's elegy on the spoiling
of the monastery at Lindisfarne,
but there was no way to capture its sorrow
and poise, Alcuin's balanced sense
of the tragic. I think this poem is about
that failure, as much as about my daughter.

2.
One who is dear to me writes of the girl
at peace in Brancusi's *La sagesse de la terre:*
"it is that kind of innate wisdom, intuitive
understanding of the right measure,
the right way, the way a child sits still
with her hands in her lap and nature is at work
in her, that quiet life-sustaining energy."
Sitting alone, my daughter sways
on the surge of a rhythm I can't hear,
her eyes closed, turned inside
to the candle gleam of void we all carry.
When she rises, it is the motion of a young doe
across a lighted space in the woods.

3.

The monks gathered without breakfast
from their meditations and sang their last matins
as the outside walls burned, their singing
punctuated by the thuds of the battering rams,
screams from the servants' quarters (I imagine),
and they saw, Alcuin says, the altar,
the goldleaf illuminations, defiled
by the *dextra ethnica,* the "heathen right hand,"
of the Danes. Similarly, in Iraq,
the soldiers were busy somewhere else
while looters took apart the National Museum.
That's the way to kill history—Sumerian
golden bulls peddled for "culture,"
or melted somewhere to cheap wedding
rings and bangles for leather bracelets.

4.

That my daughter will live in this world,
which worries her less than it worries me.
That her natural kindness could be a tincture,
a trace, as she carries herself through.
No artificial closure for these fragments:
we started out in the morning and drove
along the small, empty roads,
under sheets of early light hanging
from the branches of high trees, past
the cows and pairs of horses that turned
toward us, to the ruins, where the walls
were still crumbling, and my daughter's face
brightened, as she reached to touch the broken stone.

THE CENTER

I walked a narrow road, one side steep, dark woods,
the other a comfortless fall to a far, wasted valley.

I walked without tiring. There might have been deer
or a wolf, crouched among shadows and ferns.

It was that kind of woods, arched branches and gloom
and moss to mute footsteps, though I wasn't tempted

to leave the road and wander deeper, without aim,
as I would in real life, if this were not a dream.

Trucks hauling logs blew past, drivers annoyed
that I was there. None of them stopped to offer help.

The heavy freight rattled, swayed, and groaned,
and silence returned, richer for a bird's rare notes.

In no time, I was at the impoverished town,
rusty gas stations out of business, a hopeless factory

with painted-over windows, yards lush in weeds,
and my daughter had come to meet me, a kindness,

after years apart. In the dream, she was grown-up
and beautiful, just as she really is, and I must have been

just as I am, my beard tending to white, more
and more tremulous in my understanding of what

the world is, puzzled and often lacking for words.
We talked of children, weather, poetry, she guiding me

—toward what?—through the poor, barren streets.
Near dawn, I am telling myself a story about grace.

I've decided not to say death, though it might be so.

KIND

It is the first morning of summer, the hour when all
the tadpoles in the pond
have lost their tails, and, each the size of our son's
thumbnail, they struggle together onto land,

a synchronized swell of small flesh. It is
our boy's birthday, at six a naturalist,
and this excursion is his
requested gift, the park at dawn with both

parents, who haven't been speaking—why not
does not matter here. We've been troubled together,
and soon will be troubled apart, but now we smile
for love. Nearing the water,

he runs ahead into the over-bounty
of life. But you aren't seeing their true numbers.
Beyond any counting,
finely filed and lapidary, baby frogs suffuse

every palm's-width, a thousand on the muddy
verge of the water, ten
thousand in the seething grass. They wiggle
and hop. The short grass shivers like a skin,

and he is deep in their midst
before he understands what he is walking on
and stops, frozen still, afraid to risk
another crushing step, for even retreat

would mean slaughter now. He looks back at us
in dismay, a boy of tender
affections, his lower lip beginning to tremble.
We know how he cried when The Crocodile Hunter

was pierced to the heart, how moping and grim
he was when his hermit crabs died like clenched fists.
My then-wife says, "Get him,"
and she is right, what else but wade through that teeming

and lift his small, warm weight against my chest?
I know some of the sorriest things about death,
and he will have to learn, but I'm glad to let
our boy wait for the truth,

that any gem-perfect little frog doesn't mean much
to those spewers of spawn in their multitudes.
I carry him back to us,
killing dozens for him, and taking the blame.

The Discovery of Bread

My son was nine. We searched the bakery shelves
for the fancy, artisanal loaves he craved,

bread dense with whole grains of oat or rye,
honey-sweet, warm with imbraided garlic cloves,

crusts glinting with cracked nuggets of salt,
the savors of a richer world than he had known.

I want to tell you how he spoke the word,
careful in touching it, since asking might be

too much to risk, desire an offense, an error,
standing shy in the kitchen of his newly divorced,

and so newly strange, father's house, a boy
just learning the hints of the body his mother

and I had made for him. You must know this:
the archetypes of nourishment were sickness

to his flesh, nausea and ache, sensitivity
so accurate that pinpoint drops of milk

from someone else's spilled glass once seared
a row of crimson welts onto his bare arm,

that one bite of scrambled egg caused vomiting,
that he had grown cautious from the betrayals

of so much meant to nurture. But that year
we found some kinds of bread he could eat,

knowledge that a small good thing was possible.
Can you imagine how I loved the loaves

we bought together? We were planning dinner,
and he said, *Could we just go and get some bread?*

And so he would say *bread.* I won't say *prayer,*
but know his mouth awkward with pleasure,

humbled in asking such a word to become his flesh.

After a Commencement

The parents have grown smaller and aware.
The parents have nodded grimly

at each other's bafflement, as the apotropaic
smoke of names cleansed the stage,

invoking a polished future replete with loves
and money and ambiguous inventions,

as the past dwindles small enough to hide
with one hand. The parents swallow.

They have grown smaller and aware that inside them
are gaps and colorless matter light

has never touched. It's hard to focus at times.
There are political absurdities.

And all month, in Hawaii, volcanoes have bloomed
in dreams of primal chaos. Most

of the parents have not visited Hawaii. Some have,
briefly. Now they stretch upward

for photographs and drape their arms across
the shoulders of vast children in royal

purple gowns, children who have learned more
than anyone used to know.

We're not children, they say. Ritual has shielded
the parents from dread. Speeches and jokes,

the earnest girl with her cello, have managed the time
and delayed their dread. Happiness

helps, as long as it lasts. They think of the ancient
Higgs bosons, faithfully dimpling

space to create mass, which has happened during
their entire lives and during all

lives. In each breath, they re-cycle molecules
tasted by Caesar and Christ. The young

go off to parties, flinging their square hats
as if releasing geometric birds.

The parents drive away from the desert of crowds,
across the desert of the city outskirts,

the desert of asphalt and the terrible interrogation
of big-box hangars of unattractive

things to buy, then a highway through the desert
of medicated farmland, fields

of new, straight-ruled, trembling corn and fallow
fields like puzzled wombs made pretty

with weeds—an image the parents must reject
for now, as pathetic fallacy,

as weakness—then the desert where nomads'
fires begin to flicker in the dusk.

PART THREE

FIRST LINES OF A BREVIARY

Nearing All Hallows

There never has been anything new to say
in this great sentimental theatre.

The trees rust and bleed,
which is a luxury.

Wind strokes them, profligate
and seducing,
and hooks leaves from their branches,
undressing the scaffolds
in pain and shivering pleasure,
as when a child tears away scabs.

Wind searches me, too, wanting
to blow open the small black door
where I have hidden
a few simple things.

Winter is ahead,
beautiful pencil sketches
on bright paper.

Spring will happen when the sun pulls
all flesh pale and wet
through a narrow
aperture.

It will hurt.

The Wish Not to Move

He stands, a column of fragments, tall, falling,
and loves the unstill disquiet of February,
this distance from the floral throb of March:
wind-broken lake where water at the line
of ice is colder, more impoverished,
than ice, these raw, worried clouds, slate-gray,
spit-pale, pearlescent half-shine of burn scars
in the ache of heatless sun that limns their edges.

Day drags a thinning scrim of last night's snow
across the months-old, still unbroken crust,
a sustained sibilance that sharpens or slurs
as the wind rises or slacks, and is meaningless,
not even the terse, shrieked consonants of gulls
to liven it with their bright, famished cruelty.

FIRST LINES OF A BREVIARY

I don't know how to know
if it matters—any of it,
even the steady-into-life

of early June, when suddenly
there are oak leaves as broad
as a hand, and the purple scrota

of slipper orchids buzz
with insects—but two hardass,
fuckyou crows brawl, growling,

above the clearing, slashing
at each other for room,
with the whole fat-clouded sky

swinging around their shoulders.
Their shadows tumble below
like black gloves that try

to scrub the blood stain
of bloom from warm stones
where moss has clenched and opened

in countless crimson threads
knotting into spore, and none
of it depends on my sadness.

REALPOLITIK

The woods are beaten jagged.
The wind has snapped saplings
at mid-trunk—hundreds,
as thick as my thigh—and
flung them. An out-of-season
thunderstorm, and the road
to the dam gleams in the dove-
and-pearl, born-again morning,
broken wood polished
by breaking, as if belief
were an easy matter of the will.
Ahead, a meeting of realists—
a turkey buzzard, tented
over a flattened skunk,
shrugs into the purified air
at my approach, talons
swinging a red length of gut,
which the skunk no longer needs.

Walking the Highway Back into Town

Insects unstitch bodies in the weeds:
a possum on its back, the pads of its feet

turned up pink, an infant's supplicant palms;
a fresher possum, draped with a fertile tangle

of black and green flies; a raccoon simplified
by heat and time to a tattered pelt and a snarl

twisted to bite the tires that killed it.
Drivers honk or yell, not to warn

but telling the happy news that they are riding—
traffic from the casino that simmers with money

like fortunate blood—while others trudge in sweat
and mosquitoes, among the slain, displaced

and liable to damage. Then the poor streets.
Young men glare, astonished by their rage.

Sticky children plague a sulking, blotch-faced
woman who clouts one from a chipped porch.

The drunken, white-haired man spilling helpless
as ashes from his raveled suit wants to talk

about storm clouds thickening over the lake.
One teen-aged, dark-skinned girl stands

untouched on a high concrete wall, looking out
at what is coming, not down at us, beautiful, alone.

The Day After We Sold the World

Two-inch shoots of corn lift from the cracked mud
of fields deep in flood a week ago.
Life doesn't stop. This is comfort or warning or both.

Beside the trail, the water for long stretches
is suffused, almost too washed in light to see
as it soughs and blurs over stone,

because it is noon, and the sun comes straight
down, soaking the ravine, rather than slanting in
and pouring the hollow full of shadows, as it will later.

Water-striders skitter and pause, skitter
and pause, dimpling the surface, and frogs
kick like mad as they swim below them.

I am here, too. I sit above the waterfall, don't think,

but watch a blacksnake, this beautiful genius,
insinuating up the middle of the stream, winding
against the current, from far down, a bit of dark rope

or muscular, inky brush stroke loose
in the invisible flow, above its shadow twisting
like smoke on the pale-yellowish slate of the streambed,

curling as it sways through patches
of shade and sun, up to the falls, and out
onto a ledge beside the foam to stretch and bask.

I go home, and a gray catbird hops along the porch rail.

The Old Age of Cain

1.
My forehead, where a Mercy somewhat like lightning
leaned its thumbprint, seldom aches these days,
the mark still legible but no worse than the bruise
from stumbling into a doorframe.

2.
My name has multiplied, the generations
coming relentlessly, to this old-fashioned mind
shaped in the unteeming, primordial dawn.
I watch the young raise cities, iron smelters
and captains of work-crews, my issue,
makers of railways, tanks, bombs, colonization, financial networks,
and final machines whose wiry brains hum.

I see where this is headed.
In a culture driven from the soil, guilt
will be one of those paper fists that fall
from branches, releasing its torrent of wasps
—but who heeds the worries
of a relic whose chief fame is for murder?

3.
I find music most redemptive of my children's contrivances,
the quick, useful evolution of instruments in taut strings and tubes.
Listening, I close my eyes and tune my breathing
to taste some hint in complex harmonics
of the broken order that might have lasted.

4.
"Come home. Perhaps all might be forgiven,"
Mother writes, as mothers will,
and I am tempted—after all, I hardly remember
the green angers of baffled youth, and if I think of Abel,

it isn't my rage in the field;
I see two children, having slipped off from parents
back to the forbidden gate of Eden, daring each other
to breach the flaming sword, the grinning angel—

but I do recall Father's face dark with rage
and disappointment, shaking, lowered to the earth
over that still body.
How awkward it would be, both of us
obstinate old men now, no words
between us for too many years.
But she never surrenders hope, as mothers won't.

5.
I haven't heard from Seth in years.
He likes to tell strangers that he's an only child,
but all the strangers he meets carry me in their cells.

6.
Life goes on, as long as it does.
When Lamech kills and brags of killing,
I keep my own counsel.
I read, when music cloys, some history or books on the new physics.
I putter about in my little garden, in a straw hat for the sun
(sun irritates the mark),
whisper "brother" and "keeper" when I thump the melons for ripeness,
and walk out at night beneath stars
ever rushing away into the void like a vast gasp.
I understand this.
I invented dark matter.

EMPIRE

Night, late winter in ragged country,
a low-slung sports car punched through the dark
past starved soybean fields
and brown, wind-whipped woodlots.

You have to watch for deer.
There are always deer along that road,
their eyes flashing back
to your headlights above stretched, nervous bodies.

Sometimes you can't miss them. That is nobody's fault.
A deer stepped out of the trees in front of this driver,
and after the blow it lay broken on the asphalt,
a shattered leg, a dislocated shoulder.

The man got out and stood cursing down.
A clouding eye rolled up to him.
Breath worked loudly. Instead of killing the deer
cleanly—shooting it,

if he had a gun in the car, or finding
a heavy stone in the fallen leaves
of the nearby oaks, putting his foot
on its throat and leaning merciful weight—

he turned and got a can of gasoline,
doused the deer, flicked a match into the gasp of heat.
He drove away as the live deer burned.
The rest is a kind of baleful music.

The deer can't rise but squeals
high and thin like torn metal.
Its flesh shivers madly as the flame drills in.
Chaotic light plays shadow-and-bright

across the stoic faces of the standing trees.
Wind blunders across the whickering puddle of fire,
which grows small as a star
in the driver's rear view, if he glances back.

Promise

It looks a raw and hurting thing, deformed,
half-skinned by claws, and it squirms

with many legs—as much impulsive mercy
as disgust in my urge to stomp its misery.

It has dropped from the mower I pulled from the shed
and now struggles back toward the shade,

across asphalt, into the unkempt, seeding grass.
I don't kill it, trying these days for gentleness,

so I humble my reflex and stoop to see up close.
It isn't one creature but a mother mouse

with four hairless pups latched to her teats,
hanging on as she labors, their eyes squeezed

against the light, a tender tracing of veins
beneath the translucent, birth-pink skins,

almost beautiful. Almost. What is a burdened mother
but a warm device for stamping life on matter,

the crest of a wave of births? But don't think
this an epiphany, unless you want to call instinct

love, as it shelters the young in nurturing dark,
an energy through her, herself the pulse of its work.

Blind jaws pumping at dugs, each unresting mouth
a world, she bears their hunger back to the earth,

into a secret hollow where they can grow.
These four will be hundreds, will rut and gnaw.

NESTING

Exposed, the rabbit's nest seems almost
obscene, four squinch-eyed, naked kits,
the shallow, grass-lined nest itself a sexual
duct of the earth. They pulse and try
to squirm away from the piercing sun.

He stops the engine. He has been wrestling
the mower as it labors and chews,
levering the blades one square at a time
into the dank, seeding green, tangled
with blue chicory and thistle stalks.

Might the mother, nearby in the weeds,
carry them to safety? Is she watching,
her worry unfathomable? He dismisses
shoebox houses and medicine-droppers of food,
knowing wild things must live wild lives.
Let's say there is nothing he can do.
Bending, he touches a back, the skin as soft
as milk, and the kit quivers and knows.

Wiping the sweat of his brow, guilt
like a small stone in his throat, he leaves
them alive and waiting for fate, yanks
the cord hard and attacks the next row.

Wise crows preach from trees above his work,
perched against the sky, certain about the world.

THE DEBT

Last fall, a bear dragged a hunter from a cabin window.
He had no shocked chance to fight; it has not yet let go.
His whole head in its mouth, he heard the teeth
scraping his skull, blood spattering leaves.
It ruined him like a deer's spine, shook him hard,
but didn't kill him. He is thinking of that bear,
right now, doddering and rubbing his scars.

Fall again, the bear has no memory of the man.
The bear humps across a road in a slouchy run,
more like a big black duffel bag the wind heaves
along than an *anima loci* or ravening beast,
with eyes like heads of nails and a snout-splitting grin.
The bear basks in sun and loves its own skin
like an old hound by a stove. Deep in the thick bush,
where no person ever comes or knows, the bear pushes
over a rotting stump and mauls the soft wood, splinters
and brown punky chunks flying over its shoulders,
then squats on its haunches among the bronzed ferns
and snuffs up chubby grubs and the pale, sweet worms,
smacking its lips, farting with pleasure. At the root
of its brain, sleep starts to tighten like a knot.

This bear smells the honey of your innards, could gut
you red and gaping with one casual swipe.
It has never heard of money. You can't buy your life.

Garden, Late in Summer

If you have a garden and a library, you have all you need.
– Cicero

1.
The ivy isn't thinking about anything,
but I think it is thinking of the sea.
The wild has learned what usefulness can mean,
so the yard tries to supply nothing useful.
This busy, wet-gemmed morning after rain,
grasshoppers swaying on the climbing vines
along the fence, the square of grass and weeds
breathes and opens and stirs toward the sun,
and no use in it, nothing in the fuzzy stalks
of mullein that is fit to reap or mine.

2.
These lives are not what I decide they are.
A pair of bees fumble the dandelions,
a hunting wasp inspects the ruins of clover,
a butterfly, its yellow less lemony
than sulfur, finds ways through the maze of air,
a beetle tugs at crumbs—and each of these,
each cinched stitch snipped free from nothingness
and buzzing around the sole idea of itself,
knows one particular hunger and no word
for *bee* or *wasp* or *beetle* or *butterfly*.

3.
This is not myth, not art or engineering.
A wind insinuates beneath the ivy
to toss the leaves and let them go in muscled
undulation and susurrus along
the length of fence, which was, in winter calm,
all stark and unsymbolic characters
of brown string twisting through the wire mesh,
and now has grown again into a wall
of green that shines with red stems and pale flowers,
a shelter for flycatchers and common sparrows.

4.
Here is refuge from use. The great agendas
murmur far away like waves on stone.
Buddha, Jesus, and Einstein have given themselves
to free the thistle that grows rich with neglect.
A robin turns the corner of the house,
blurs past, so close I hear the *swash* of wings,
and perches on the toolshed's shingled roof.
It plucks a note to test the neighborhood,
an echo where the sky spirals small,
three warm ounces around a trilling throat.

Imagine a Woman Behind Razor Wire

– after a photograph by Cheryl Dodds, "Railroad Diary, Istanbul, 2012"

1.
A long time ago, when we lived in the sky....

2.
But no, we invented that because of pain,
because desire tortures even the dirt and stones into division,
into definition fracture power solitude wall razor wire.

3.
(But pleasure is also real. Joy is real. One autumn day, my wife
climbed a fence and stole from a farmer's disregarded field,
knotty tart small apples burnished by the wind and the sun,
and she gave me one, though I watched her eat and tasted her mouth, instead.
Not everyone remembers that such things are possible, since they often happen
only once.)

4.
"Razor wire" is a slang term. Did you know that?
Industry professionals call it "barbed tape,"
like something your father would carry in his toolbox.

5.
If you receive no beatings, how do you know who you are?

6.
I insist on saying this plainly, without art:
if you remember joy, you must tell it speak it write it.

7.
Once I found someone's voice lying on the ground,
a little puddle or puzzle of utterances, desperate
and wet and confused by having been cut or torn from a warm throat.
I brushed it off, and it huddled against the inside of my hand,
nuzzling for safety. I held it to my ear,
and it was like the sea shouting in the vast rooms of a shell,
yet not like that, not at all.

8.
Imagine a woman standing behind razor wire,
glimpsed, as you pass to your easy life.
This poem is not the gift of a woman's voice.
See how external I have remained, despite certain maneuvers
that I hoped would bring me closer?
This poem is white noise leaning into silence.

The Ugly Flower: a Science Fiction Story
....an I slipped away into dumbness.
—Paul Celan, "Homecoming"

In this myth from the ancient world, there was a home
with many houses in it, some shaded by leaves

in summer, then warm with the pleasures of going to bed
in winter. Others were different. We nomads of the stars

were small then, implied in the cells of the ancients.
(Let the voice that says the poem say "I was there.")

One heard whales breaching off the coast,
and insects busy in the sexual chambers of plants.

There were islands and ferns, museums and mitochondria,
hard to choose the right details when all are right,

and because many important things had no names,
and, even so, the named beings were beyond count,

rather than the 257 that exist now.
When the clutter and pulse were dying,

burning, buried under made things, veins clotted,
no more whales ever, the ancients gathered

for what they called "the great leap," out into
the maybe-nothing, the maybe-somewhere,

snug in their flung cradles
that rocked them into the new

—but the voice that says "I" in the poem,

I pause at the gate and look out into the vast, prosperous shine.
I smile with a sadness that seems remembered, or a memory

that seems a sorrow, and turn back. I walk long in the soot,
until I find a wildflower of a kind never noticed before,

a gray, misshapen bloom, clinging to the ground. I sit beside
my sister flower and croon our names and wait for the fire.

KAIROS

A moth, rich with detail as a Dürer engraving,
               is trapped in the house, weak

from batting windows.
               Ash-gray with shocked

mahogany eye spots,
               the wings sag from exhaustion,

twitch once as my hands
               close over them, and relent,

settle to any doom
               in the warm vault of capture.

The wings brush my palms like eyelashes.
               Thrown from the dim room

to raw noon sun,
               the moth loops and staggers

in jagged, drunken orbits,
               until it finds a shaded crevice

to shelter from the harsh mercy
               of rescue, tilting through

this vertigo of color,
               this chaos of brightness,

blinded from sifter of night
               to a throbbing eye by that instant,

salt-white scouring we all desire and dread,
               the shine of a day

when even the dark will burn.

Near Sleep

Whenever wind leans on
the walnut tree, it brushes

a few nuts loose, the strikes
muffled and close, a hammer

underground, unmaking
the walls of a bad year.

Spring mornings, luna moths
sheltered there, walking

the undercurves of branches,
clever swatches of green silk

spun from leaves and fog
like ideas about an afterlife.

Now, between world and dream,
I pick one up, let it wander

the back of my hand, hesitating,
wings soft as the inside of an eyelid.

Our Abandonment

Between spring and summer, we saw that the rapture had already happened.
Some of us went from house to house
to learn who was gone.
Not many, as it turned out.

Flowers functioned.
The trillium and toadlilies made way
for the plump, purple seductions of slipper orchids.
Bees labored in the heat, as always,
and coddled sweetness from the noxious honeyvine.
Birds left their clutches of emptied shells.

We didn't know if this continuance would matter.
Maybe it would,
but, since the meanings were all in the past,
would it matter that it mattered?

Children were unable to hold the losses strictly in their minds,
so they ventured outside, joined hands,
played in the yards and on the asphalt,
tossing balls, inventing complicated, hermetic figures with chalk.

Autumn came,
and we lay at night and waited as the swell of wind
tore loose the old leaves,
and they rushed away,
as if drawn into the gasping maw of a distant blaze.

Now, the first snow surprises me.
I look up into the shifting swirl,
the air sharpened into separate points of cold,
and the flakes melt on my face.

Do you see this, bereft ones?

Brief Turns of Weather

1
Midday, warm for this early March, hovers
above ice, as wind thins through paltry weeds

in cracks of asphalt and makes them tremble.
Coatless, I loiter along the driveway

to know wind, slate-dour sky and frozen yard.
Grey rain alternates with *corna cealdast,*

the phrase from a frost-bitten north
girding curt pellets with sower's irony.

They sizzle on earth, these "coldest of seeds,"
that won't root here, that rain will wash to slush,

though nearby, dark in sod beneath the freeze,
shoots curl tight in sheaths, test the loam, nudge.

2.
Popcorn snow was my mother's name for this,
as much for the look of flakes compact as hail

as for their rattle and bounce off stiffened ruts.
Winter always began with it, after wires

of rime had bound the wasted leaves to mud,
as gusts trapped in snarls of pale sedge

beat themselves free and thrust birds sideways.
The day the weather turned, the fall's first white

like shot stinging the backs of hands, shushing
among corn stubble, we were binding the rustle

of foddershocks and stopped to gauge the sky.
"A foot by morning," she judged and stooped to the work.

79

But I'm no farmer now. It has been decades
since I leaned cornstalks in shocks for fodder

or gathered armfuls to winter a milk cow.

3.
I watch the shifting flakes define dimensions
with a Lucretian randomness of swifting,

blown swirl—just as, one June, I stood
with my wife under the broad, innocent maple

that shivered once, or seemed to shiver in pleasure,
and released its shower of blossoms down on us,

as pale and swerving as snow-petals, glittering
as they found slants of light that pierced the shade.

4.
Remember, love? We took the path beyond
litter and road noise, through waist-tall ferns

into the cooler woods, and then that clarity
of falling petals, a space where silence held,

as if, unknowing, we had stepped into an air
outside the seasons, breath stilled between breath

and breath. You gripped my hand, so I would pause
for once from my world-long stumble, look up

to find the maple flowers in timeless drift.

5.
And we knew the place already. Earlier,
at the gray edge of spring, a day like this

of mist and restless cloud, we climbed rock
and sat talking on wet lichen, and we shivered

out of our clothes, your cry an echo over stone,
both timeless and the quick of pure happening.

6.
This snow is ending already, no real threat
in these brief squalls, and soon the softened loam

will ruck open where life rises to thrust
hungrily at the day, as Pound observed,

naming "the gilded phalloi of the crocuses."
I like the thought, this sexual, seeded earth,

but hear a cheating fall in "gilded."
I'd rather gold, or, better still, pure flame.

7.
In no hurry, a buzzard lifts and lifts
above the neighbor's plowed field, describing

time's other spiral, brown flap of canvas
lofted away from earth. I turn from watching sky,

fissures of blue in the banked marl of cloud.
I am younger now than the crocus shoots.

PART FOUR

ONTARIO

Vivaldi: *Cello Concerto in D Minor, RV 406*

Like relief when she steps from the door-
way, face and hair adept with falls of sun

through late shadows of leaves.
If he were air, if he were music.

In the deepening mood of long past noon,
there are moments like the lighted pause

between movements of a concerto,
spacious and stilled into her grace,

a hold for gathering breath, then the turn,
release, those first notes a new arrival.

JEWISH GRAVES, NORTHERN ONTARIO
....snowfall, as if even now you were sleeping.
—Paul Celan, "Homecoming"

The world and I have wandered here and stopped. Some days a fox trots
between the headstones from woods to woods, the pocked trunks of aspens

where stubborn leaves still hush the wind as first flakes of snow swerve down,
and two crows patrol overhead, low enough that I hear the *swash swish*

their wings brush on quiet, so I forgive the plastic flowers that have forgotten
where they belong, blown scuttling from grave to grave, no respect for borders.

The cemetery here is one side Protestant, meaning mostly the curt granite
of 19th century whisky-and-brogue Scots who engineered roads and sunk mines

into the Precambrian Shield. Then the Catholic side is split again,
English and French, and one odd corner an awkward leftover of the puzzle,

a half-dozen graves fenced off for the Greenburgs and Silvermanns
who sold dry goods and groceries in the patchwork town, turn of the last

century, after the fur trade had died but before nickel and uranium, when logs
glutted and clacked in the river's throat. There are no Jews in town now. It
        seems

they settled in raw country just long enough to lodge these dead, then retreated
east or pushed west. The newest grave is from the nineteen-thirties, but
        someone visits

and balances pebbles atop the worn markers. For example

    Regina Silvermann
    beloved daughter
    of Aaron and Rosie
    b. July 1898 d. Aug 1899

—thirteen months of unimaginable life, infant pleasures and hungers, waking to
tears and milk, guessing the first words for desire. Then a few, persistent ounces
      of dust,

and the unceremonious snow has shrouded her one hundred and nineteen times.
Generations of foxes have printed that blankness, and the thin pencil—

sketchings of the aspens' shadows, when they lengthen on afternoons
of winter sun, inscribe no message I can read, as illegible as relief or refuge.

I favor this section on my strolls among the dead, drawn to the weathering stars
carved in rock, square-charactered verses my bumbling un-knowledge

can't decide to call frost-chipped Hebrew or Yiddish. I'd like someday to lie here
among these displaced ones, if that were not breaking a *mitzvah*—

it seems right a stranger might be gathered to strangers, all of us belonging
where we don't belong, eased at last into our unease on the brief earth.

Eᴘɪᴄ Sɪᴍɪʟᴇ

I thought that day of Baudelaire's *éphémère*,
which flies at a candle, crackles, burns, and prays,

"Bless this torch." It was the obvious thought
in the mostly empty scrap of town, hanging on

somehow, at the lake's edge, as autumn pushed
a slate-grey swell that made the floating docks

grieve in their chains and drove the tourists south.
Another month would ice the lake to silence,

but we walked the unresting border hand-in-hand,
past the rotting fish where furious, turning

gulls descended to thrust their heads into flesh
or shrieked on beating wings to warn us off.

We climbed stairs to the street: the Evangelist
lonely on stained glass, a lagging bait-and-tackle,

the out-of-business general store. We shaded
our eyes to peek inside at shelves of cans

and dusty knick-knacks losing cheer in the dimness,
and, at the end of the concrete porch, what looked

like leaves blown there and matted rank with damp
was really the bodies of moths, hundreds of moths,

blond layers as thick as a pillow full of sleep,
under a bare bulb, always lit, a glowing trap.

Years later, I think of Homer's helpless grief,
the Achaeans who rushed at Ilion in mad desire

and fell from light to strew the blood-fed ground.

Cycle, Then Stasis

A man waits at a table between the lake and the museum,
shuttered since tourists escaped this poor town for fall,

and a cormorant tacks back and forth a few meters
from shore, diving and coming up unpredictably,

straying beneath the sombering images of sky and cloud
for what seems an impossible term, before its dark head

bobs into sight far away. Now the man lays his face
on the table and shields it from wind under his hands.

Maybe he is tired, maybe his child is sick and he prays
without the faith he had once, begging to take her place,

maybe the whole world is bitter, or maybe he is happy,
no matter how it all looks, thinking about his wife's body.

He must still hear the couple of dozen gray-backed gulls
that loiter on a near patch of sand, shrieking as one or another

rushes the lake in a hopping run to lift off and flap
over the water in a lop-sided loop that brings it back

where it began, as if testing the weather
for some quality favorable to gulls and finding it lacking.

Beside the table, an ancient boiler from the engine room
of the fishing tug *Everad*—which, a plaque says,

pulled whitefish from the North Channel off Mudge Bay
during the 1940s—proclaims the town's useful past.

The wind shifts, and the reflected sunset shivers like flesh.
The hollow of the boiler would be large enough to sleep in.

BUYING FROM THE MENNONITES

The summer is long, fields tightening like tanning hides
beneath the weight of lye-and-ashes sky
August sun rubs into them, corn sparse and slant,
but wheat a copper-gold weave the wind strokes

to a ground-level shimmer around the tufts.
The farmhouse sits back along a lane of shade trees.
I am here for eggs, tomatoes, other garden things.
Silence, except wind and a red-winged blackbird

spalling notes off the block of quiet. The farmer nods
from the shed where he is planing curls from a board,
in a shirt and vest, in this heat, to honor the work.
His wife meets me on the porch, three tables

spread with peas and peppers and broccoli,
hair tucked beneath her bonnet, dress to her ankles.
She holds her eyes lowered, her only words *hello*
and *thank you*. She looks tired from repeated work.

Circled on her own thoughts, she goes in for the eggs,
and I—a trespass, a cliché—imagine their blue twilights
together, far from town, almost in secret out here,
the first coolness settling dust, as labor eases

from muscles, her curves suddenly dusk-lit pale
as the dress falls. Does she raise her all-day-disciplined
eyes, both man and woman revealed and lovely now,
and more so for limit, for restraint and release?

She comes back and leans over the tomatoes to choose
for me, and the light flakes just right off their red
and yellow skins, playing on her dress as she reaches, on throat
and forehead, like the glow on one tending a bed of embers.

The Farmer Wakes to the Sound of Good Weather

Rain drubs clean his dust-clogged veins.
Its roar thrums in, through still-dark,
sleep-vague dawn around his head,
revels now in the drought-grogged dream,
drunk on cloudburst and mudthought
in all his flesh. He dreams he is the field
long coaxed by prayerstick fingers.
The dirt's need floods him. Rain heals
cracked soilskin, silks into crannies,
unknotting clods. Leaves uncrease,
uncurl from their wither. It rewebs
his frame in a fine weave of sprouts.
He yawns, stretches crouch-cramped limbs,
feels the tender cornshoots saved on his chest,
knows lettuce drinking sweetly at his palm.

Inukshuks

Only camping tourists make them now.
I've grumbled about that urge to own

a mirror in the bush, to erect a center
so the wild must fall into civil rank

around the builder. Farther north,
serious stone men once stood sentinel

over caribou runs and turned meat
toward the spears, but these are play,

toddler-tall, a feckless gathering lifted
to balance from river rock, on a bank left dry

through summer, though the rise after autumn rain
will drown them. Ice will crack their chests.

But for miles of tamarack and wind I've heard
no voice, so I go down in the evening shade

to touch the stones some other has touched,
to set a tumbled few back upright and nod

a private word of solace to each, water-
smooth and day-warm, welcome to the hand.

Poem Ending with an Imitation of a Line from Philippe Jaccottet

Hold this. Windows down, throwing strawberry stems
from the car, you and I drive the ruts by Cutler Lake,
moaning with pleasure as the sun-sugared berries
shiver, burst, and dissolve, the best just now starting to blet.

Hold this. A goldfinch flits and dodges. We scent woodsmoke
like foreknowledge of autumn. And swathes of the cold water,
watching wisely through birch trunks as we skirt the shore,
are as dark-sifting blue and deep-memoried as soot.

Hold this. Just as you lift a bitten berry by the stem
to praise, "It's like drinking life from a goblet,"
I ask, in the dim guard booth at the top of my spine,
some wordless question that might translate as "Why death?"

For answer, from the roadside: *vetch, trefoil, curled dock.*

The Only Arts are Music and Loss

We find theme and variation at the trees' edge,
each a singular wave offering water and earth
to the sun at peculiar angles only crows know,
or sloughing twilight from their branches,

and she is a wave, too, lifting her portion of earth
and breath, an energy, a clean curve in time
more beautiful even than her body, the gorgeous debris
she carries through the air. We knew those trees,

the breaks in cloud cover
that played afternoon light over the fields
like the rhythm of fingertips on a lover's back,
on a lover's pulse. That night she cried,

seeing the impossibility of holding each pine or birch
in mind, each note shining on the trunks.
How perfect our loss then, crest and breaking,
that beauty we would not choose.

MARRIAGE

We had seen wolves before, and more often
heard a pack hunting, but this wolf

was alone at the end of a grave winter,
fur matted in poor tufts, as it cringed

across the packed snow of the path
up ahead, looked back at us, and faded

into the trees. Sick or hurt,
starving, but still with muscle like coiled cable

beneath its loose fell, still with teeth,
still better at living in the cold than we are,

it passed silently, broad paws on top of the snow,
and I saw what was in that glance back:

a gauging of the odds. Our voices
stopped, and by instinct we drew closer together.

We were two, but if either of us
had been one, the wolf might have turned

to that solitary flesh, driven brave by famine.

A RED SCRIM OF BUDS ON THE DISTANT TREES

After all that happened, my new wife and I park beside a river
dark and risen with the runoff from melting snow.

We stuff cold-reddened hands into jacket pockets
and walk a boot-packed trail through birch woods,

past a deserted farmhouse relaxing into its cellar,
a heavy animal that has floundered here

and acquiesces as the earth takes it back.
Before long the snow will let go, ferns will thrust

watery shoots through the mat of old fronds,
migratory birds will throw their colors through the shade.

We stand together on a wooden footbridge and look down
into water black with the end of winter, the stream swelling

over its banks, shimmering intricately as it braids
the flattened brown reeds and loosens thin skirts

of broken ice around the stems of weeds,
juncos bobbing from bush to bush and skittering

in the ground cover, the gray air fallen over
everything like the sheerest possible mesh

threatening to tangle itself into snow again.
We kiss. I love her warm mouth.

Pussy willows push their white tufts into the day.
Buffleheads rise from the river and skim their images toward shore.

After Reading "Mourning and Melancholia," I Go for a Walk

1.
The evening is cool after rain.
Among the puddles that gleam
under the chain-link fence
of the dairy processing plant,
I meet a frog half the bulk of my hand
and guide him off the road, into grass,
so he can go on eating and rutting.
Men and women are beginning
a shift beside the pasteurizing vats.
Later tonight, I think around three a.m.,
a young Anishinaabe woman
might step out onto a loading dock
for a break from the sour breath
of hot milk and might hear crickets
and the aching, lovely, clacking passage
of a slow train that comes
and leaves without stopping,
far on the other side of Highway 17.

2.
Now I walk by the rich houses
that afford views above the river,
many yards with FOR SALE signs.
I move quietly, without envy.
I've only ever stolen one thing,
as far as I recall—a book,
a worn, water-stained copy
of Marlowe's *Doctor Faustus*
when I was eighteen years old,
and I spent a fine morning reading,
in my parents' sunlit back yard,
guiltless, delighted, knowing
nothing of what would come.
Is *not knowing* what I have lost,
since I must have lost something?

3.
Before circling back to lamps
and sleep, I touch the stations
of my way through town,
the bulldozed lot where for years
a derelict house thrived like a lung
with the tholing tones of pigeons,
another house where Mrs. Gross
lived with her son while Alzheimer's
sleeked her as innocent as untrodden
earth, and the bridge where my wife
met a wolf at night, two winters ago.
He bulked real and stiff-footed
in the middle of the road and watched
her face, awaiting his chance.
It was snowing. Just beyond
the final light, more shapes
slouched hungry from the dark.
She backed away, slow, too wise
to run, and came breathing home.

At Summer's Decline

This rain never tires. I am unsteady today,
but I go out in a fever, no metaphor,
a real cling of heat fogging my skin,
some muzzy dread throbbing above my eyes.

A month ago, to seal a day of brassy sun,
we swam a secret pool in the forest,
where at eye-level small curls of mist
licked the cooling air, and my wife,

rising from a dive, turning to me,
gathered the rare light and wore it.
Now, a drowned mole shines in the puddle
between the bent roots of a big oak,

fur sleek, clean as broken anthracite.
Five wild turkeys drip as they cross the path.
Rain shivers over my heat like pleasure,
weather a numb drone in the trees.

Tapestry, I think, as a meadow rustles,
thistle sewn into the rank tangle
of ragweed. As if that word would lift
it all. As if it needed to be lifted.

Your Husband Thinks of You from an Autumn Day in the Better Life

He could fix his gaze
on the algae-slicked sides of stumps
waterlogged black among weeds

or notice how the dull gloss of the day lingers
on detail, pad and claw of a small animal's
sharp prints across wet sand,

ending where wind-driven ripples
ruffle up and slack down, retreat,
and erase the farthest pair of tracks,

but the pale ribs and thighs of birch
gleam among tamarack on the other shore
and call him across the fifty-yard

reach of unstill, iron-gray water.
He wants to stand and walk to the trees,
glance back and see this shore dwindle,

a small, lighted room
glimpsed through a distant door
whose life he could cover with a raised palm,

and for a few beats he is back in those years,
and if he starts to sink, he will pull water
cold into his chest like nightfall and will sink.

But instead he remembers the last breath
before meeting you, the steps barefoot
across carpet to your knock,

the last step and pause at the door
where you waited on the other side,
that final moment of the old life

when the two of you stood face
to face like lovers, not touching yet,
though the only barrier left to solve

was two inches of blank wood and a lock.

Woman in Sunlight

That day the river lay as beautiful
as a woman on her lover's bed,
if a woman's flanks could shine
the way sunlight caressed the water,

and she and I—the real woman,
not the river—climbed from the water
dripping, to eat bread and fruit
and lie on moss beneath the trees,

trying to take as much of the sky
as possible into our eyes. Spirit—
it seemed the bread in our hands
might verge into spirit, so lucid

was the air holding us, and the trees
were finally emblems of spirit,
from the cool earth to the upper twigs
mixing with sky. The shine of a bee's wings

as it crawled unstinging over the woman's
belly became the shine
of spirit going abroad,
embodied there in sunlight

and the sun's meeting with water
and skin. Who would not want a vision
of the world where this
would be enough for the woman,

a sufficient way of speaking about life,
or of the spirit speaking for itself
in the bee exploring her belly,
dipping around the rim of her navel

and flying from between her breasts?
Imagine that sort of world.
Imagine that we watched the bee
and turned hungry toward each other.

BEWILDERMENT

A man knows himself unworthy, her love unmerited,
a mystery like a healing after a wing's light touch.
And he no longer tries to hide his failings,
humbled and as helpless for wounds
as if he were already old and almost blind
and forgets his way in a well known city.
Shaking, he takes out a worn, often folded paper,
and asks strangers to read a name, an address.

ONTARIO

The world is gone, I must carry you.
—Paul Celan

1.
Fourth grade, we were all in love with Mrs. Dale,
the pretty, dark-haired teacher, who was kind
and grew rounder under her floral dresses,
autumn to spring, as she englobed her own child,
whom she would like better than any of us.

This was in Virginia. I was one of the miners' kids
who rode the bus to school, marbles and jackknives
stuffed in our pockets, our mothers
proud of mended jackets and clean faces.

There was a jigsaw map of Canada in the classroom,
though no one had ever been there.
The finger-polished wooden provinces
clicked rightly into their slots,
golden for Saskatchewan clothed in wheat,
a cool green for forested Quebec,
Alberta purple for no good reason,
each pocked with a black dot for its capital.

I wanted north, had read *The Call of the Wild*,
so the puzzle's true goal was to imagine a way
to the Yukon and Northwest Territories,
a ground for testing some intuited question
against ice and dogs and pain.
I fitted blander sections of the nation into place
on the path to trackless snow, the Arctic sea,
bravery defined in white silence.

2.

You were on Manitoulin then, four years old,
on that hard island where, you've told me,
"a man shifts a boulder to plant a seed."
I know that you are gentler to my hungers
because of the things that happened there,
the days you carry to me and allow
to tell their dark shimmer like broken coal.

In that wooden Ontario I ignored on my way north,
I held all that you had ever seen, the day
when you ranged glazed tea figurines on the floor
of the shed, while your living father
worked around you, and the pelts of beaver
and otter and fox ticked tighter in racks on the walls.
I keep these details close: your pet duck pipping
into life from an egg beneath a lamp,
toffee softened in the sun, a girl's secret
notes hidden among the stones of a fence.

And next, when I had changed schools and lost
my North for thirty years, slow on the orbit
that would at last curve to you,
you watched your father walk into the woods,
traps slung over his shoulder, that night
of grief you didn't yet understand, boots in the light
from the doorway, men weighted silent with news,
who had been searching, cold, out in the wet darkness.

ABOUT THE AUTHOR

James Owens grew up in the coal-mining country of Appalachian Virginia, attended King College, and worked as a reporter and editor on newspapers in the region, before studying poetry at the University of Alabama and receiving an MFA in 2002. He now lives with his wife in a small town in Ontario, along the north shore of Lake Huron, where the winters are long enough to make the summers precious. He has three children and two step-children, all grown, and spends as much time as he can in the woods and near the water. Of his writing, he comments, "I try to negotiate a balance between the ecstatic possibilities of language and nature and the hard-edged boundaries of the moment." He has published widely, including three previous books of poems: *An Hour is the Doorway* (2007), *Frost Lights a Thin Flame* (2007), and *Mortalia* (2015).

ACKNOWLEDGMENTS

My gratitude to the editors of the following journals, where many of these poems have appeared, often in earlier versions.

"Lascaux" in *The American Journal of Poetry;* "Carnage" in *Appalachian Heritage;* "Nights at 7-Eleven" in *Atlanta Review;* "Nearing All Hallows" in *Autumn Sky;* "Wanting a Storm on his Birthday" in *Bangor Literary Journal;* "Sledge" in *Birmingham Poetry Review;* "Imagine a Woman Behind Razor Wire" and "The Ugly Flower" in *Blue Fifth Notebook;* "Lindisfarne" in *Canary;* "Kind" in *Chestnut Review;* "The Day After We Sold the World" on the blog of *The Dark Mountain Project;* "Walking the Highway Back into Town" in *Flying Island;* "After Reading 'Mourning and Melancholia,' I Go for a Walk" in *Good Works Review;* "Last Thoughts Cooling Like an Abandoned Cup" in *James Dickey Review;* "Near Sleep" and "Vivaldi: *Cello Concerto in D Minor, RV 406*" in *The High Window;* "A Prayer for Unison" in *Heron Tree;* "The Old Age of Cain" and "Ontario" in *The Honest Ulsterman;* "Cleave" (as "Wood") in *Now & Then;* "Empire" in *ONE;* "Kairos" in *The Other Journal;* "Buying from the Mennonites," "Family Portrait with Scythe," "The Farmer Wakes to the Sound of Good Weather" and "Story" in *Pikeville Review;* "Inukshuks" in *Relief;* "Hard Rain Behind a Screen of Thistles" in *Poetry Ireland Review;* "At Summer's Decline" and "The Prodigal Son Makes Notes for a Eulogy and Never Mentions the Fatted Calf" in *Psaltery and Lyre;* "Poem Ending with an Imitation of a Line from Phillippe Jaccotet" and "The Discovery of Bread" in *Southword;* "Abundance" in *The Sow's Ear Poetry Review;* "Marriage" in *Split Rock Review;* "Realpolitick" in *Still: The Journal;* "Bewilderment" in *Summerset Review;* "Funeral" and "A Red Scrim of Buds on the Distant Trees" in *The Sunlight Press;* "Looking Back" in *takahē;* "The News, c. 1969" and "Waking Beside a Scene from *The Inferno*" in *Town Creek Poetry;* "Light Whispers through the Skin of the World" in *Twyckenham Notes;* "Your Husband Thinks of You from an Autumn Day in the Better Life" in *Tule Review;* "Brief Turns of Weather" in *Valparaiso Poetry Review;* "Body" and "First Lines of a Breviary" in *Watershed Review;* "Scythe" in *West Texas Literary Review*

www.ingramcontent.com/pod-product-compliance
Lightning Source LLC
Chambersburg PA
CBHW031142090426
42738CB00008B/1185